Ms Blaelock's Book of Planning a Life Worth Living

Also by Alexandria Blaelock

MS BLAELOCK'S BOOKS
Stress Free Dinner Parties
Signature Wardrobe Planning
Holistic Personal Finance
Minimally Viable Housekeeping

FICTION
That Love Nonsense

SHORT STORY COLLECTIONS
The Haunting of Hayward Hall
Common or Garden Variety Heroes
Lovelorn, Lovestruck and Love and First Sight

Ms Blaelock's Book of Planning a Life Worth Living

Alexandria Blaelock

BlueMere Books
MELBOURNE, AUSTRALIA

Copyright © Alexandria Blaelock, 2021.

All rights reserved. No part of this publication may be reproduced, distributed or transmitted in any form or by any means, including photocopying, recording, or other electronic or mechanical methods, without the prior written permission of the publisher, except in the case of brief quotations embodied in critical reviews and certain other non-commercial uses permitted by copyright law.

For permission requests, contact enquiries@bluemerebooks.com.

Ordering Information:
Discounts are available on quantity purchases. For details, contact orders@bluemerebooks.com.

Ms Blaelock's Book of Planning a Life Worth Living/Alexandria Blaelock.

hardback ISBN: 978-1-925749-64-9
paperback ISBN: 978-1-925749-65-6
digital ISBN: 978-1-925749-66-3

Book Layout © 2015 BookDesignTemplates.com
Cover Image © RetroClipArt/Shutterstock.com

*In memory of my father;
the most adventurous person I know.*

The more time you spend contemplating what you should have done... you lose valuable time planning what you can and will do.

–LIL WAYNE

Contents

Introduction	1
Preparation	5
Priorities	15
Goals	21
Clarity	29
Planning	33
Tracking	41
Conclusion	47
Glossary	49
Bibliography	51
Index	53
Author's Note	54
About the Author	55

Introduction

LIFE HAS A WAY OF getting out of control.

You really want to get something done, but at the end of the day, or weekend, you haven't quite got there. Nor at the end of the week, or the end of the month.

And before you know it, another year has gone by and you still haven't done it.

Maybe you want to get a degree, but don't have four years to set aside to attend campus full-time. Perhaps smaller spaces within the fabric of your life might allow one or two units a semester; part-time or online.

Or you might want to take an overseas trip; Paris let's say. You'll need to save some money, research the best flights, accommodation and sites to visit before assembling an itinerary. Plus look into visas and any vaccinations required to visit.

Or you might decide you want to buy a house. To succeed, you'll need a deposit, mortgage finance, and some kind of plan for choosing a property in an area you can afford.

These are all long-term goals, that need to be broken into shorter-term goals. Most commonly, annual goals based on New Year's Resolutions.

Or maybe they'll be for just a month or two, like slimming down for Summer, completing NanoWriMo, or running a marathon.

You can't achieve these goals without allocating time and money to them.

And you'll need to make choices about what you're willing to let go, so you have the time and money to achieve them.

It might be that you're one of those lucky people who can give yourself a Word of the Year and do perfectly well with just that.

I can't. If I didn't incorporate structure into my life, I would never get anything done.

Or you might get along perfectly well with a cast iron set of habits, day in and day out. And if that's you, I envy you too, because I get massively derailed by the slightest thing.

This book lays out the process I use each year for my annual planning; business and personal lives.

- Lay out my Vision, Mission and Values.
- Decide my Priorities.
- Choose some Goals.
- Schedule time to "work" on them, and if necessary, set up a budget.
- Track how I'm doing.

I originally wrote parts of this book for the original *Holistic Personal Finance*, (now updated and republished as *Ms Blaelock's Book of Holistic Personal Finance*), and *Ms Blaelock's Book of Minimally Viable Housekeeping*.

This book's for people who don't want or need the financial or household management aspects, but find they need to change their life, and need help sorting through their options.

In the original books, I included some sample families, and I've left them in to give you some idea of how you can adapt the processes for your needs.

I hope you find it useful.

CHAPTER 1

Preparation

PEOPLE WHO OWN BUSINESSES ARE often very focused on generating enough income to cover their costs, plus a bit more to live on. And to do this, they often develop:

- A vision statement to describe their goal.
- A mission statement about how they're going to achieve it.
- Values to explain what drives them to achieve their mission.

These statements describe the company's core philosophy; its what, how and why. And theoretically at least, they underpin every decision made at every level, from purchasing to marketing, to employee selection.

And if you like this kind of thing, they can do a pretty good job for your personal life as well. Here's how it works.

Vision Statement

A vision statement is an expression of what your ideal universe looks like, and your place in it.

You could imagine it as your potential future. But if you want it to be inspiring and actionable, it's more useful to give it a long-term time frame of five to ten years.

For example, if you're in a "minority group" you may look for a world where all people receive equal consideration, but for your five-year time frame limit it to equal consideration under the law. Or if you hope for a world without war, hunger, or corruption, you might restrict it to your community or state.

Visions don't have to be BIG things, but they need to be big enough and inspiring enough to form a firm foundation for you to work from and towards.

It doesn't have to be A vision either. It can be a combination of ideas, as long as you can make it an inspiring and memorable statement, like a 140-character tweetable.

Life being what it is, things change often. If you marry, you might work up a joint statement as well as your own. And later have children and want a family statement to join your personal and couple statements.

Maybe you'll discover you have a terminal disease, which will change your ideas as well.

Because of events like these, we don't set and forget the vision, we review it annually.

But for the moment, just consider what you want right now. Let's take a look at what our families might say:

The Baker Family

Emily hopes to meet a nice boy and get married, but first, she wants to get her own place.

Not necessarily buy right now because she wants to pay off her student debt and travel as well, but a little place she doesn't have to share, where she can come and go as she pleases.

Her vision statement could be "I live debt-free in an inexpensive, cosy apartment with red geraniums on my window sill. My lovely neighbours water my plants when I travel."

The Smiths

Bob and Amanda are concerned about the world their children are growing up in.

The air and water are polluted, the climate is changing, and there are additives in the food. They worry about the quality of education and feel they're not living in the kind of village they want bringing up their children.

They feel a move to a more rural location might be best, somewhere with a large yard to play in, plenty of space to grow fruit, vegetables and chickens. Somewhere in a close-knit community with a good school.

The Smith vision could be "We're part of a close-knit rural community, growing healthy produce, and the children are receiving a good independent education."

The Butchers

As they approach their retirement, Ash and Jo don't feel they don't spend enough time together.

They want to nurture their relationship and pursue an activity together, perhaps cooking, or taking a Spanish class so they can travel. Maybe walk the 500 mile (790 km) Camino de Santiago, though they acknowledge they'll need to build their fitness and stamina to finish it. They'd like to have a more active role in the lives of their nieces and nephews.

Their vision statement might be "A long, happy and healthy life, enjoying indoor and outdoor activities together. Building an enormous memory bank to share with our family."

As you can see, these are different impressions of what people may hope for, reduced into a simple, memorable statement. They're not detailed enough to plan, but they're detailed enough to imagine, and this is the key component of keeping your vision alive:

The softness of your couch on your skin as you drink coffee and listen to the silence of being alone in your own home.

Hearing birdsong and the wind in the trees as you sit on your deck with your family watching the sunset.

Feeling the sun on your back, the strength in your limbs and smelling wild thyme as you walk.

Mission Statement

The mission statement turns your vision into a reality. It explains what you're going to do and why. Again, it doesn't have to be particularly detailed, it's a hint at how you'll proceed.

If your vision statement was set in five years, your mission is your three-year milestone.

It's another short, positive statement bringing your vision into reality.

"Promoting equal consideration under the law through community action, and policy advocacy."

"Ending hunger in my local community by seeking food donations and cooking at the homeless shelter."

"Helping sick animals by getting good grades and becoming a veterinarian."

"Loving God and serving people."

"Treasuring my children."

Like your vision, you may want to come up with joint or family missions as well.

Baker

"Commit to an abundant future with a spending plan to pay off debt quickly and maximise long-term savings."

Smith

"Prioritise the children's long-term interests with a healthier and happier lifestyle in a cleaner nutritive environment."

Butcher

"Treasuring our relationship by enjoying time together; getting fit, hiking in the country, cooking and speaking Spanish."

Virtues Statement

With your vision (big picture) and mission (medium size picture) taken care of, it's time to zoom in closer and think about what's important to you.

The way I see it, the fundamental goal of life is increasing happiness and decreasing unhappiness. I don't mean happiness in the sense of a good mood, but the feeling of well-being that comes from enjoying a life you think is worth living.

Ancient Philosophers called this "flourishing"; an awareness of growing and developing, reaching to become something more than you were before. It might be "serving your country", "making glorious art" or something else. And the resulting feeling may be satisfaction, pleasure or similar.

Knowing the activities and people who are important to you, and focusing on them, gives you the opportunity to create a fuller, richer and happier life.

You may have heard the expression "a means to an end" or perhaps a debate about whether "the end justified the means". The end is the result you want, and the means the way you get there.

The means/ends debate comes from the moral philosophy of Immanuel Kant (1724 - 1804). He argued that people are valuable because they are people (an end in themselves), not tools (the means).

So, if you'd like to visit the Eiffel Tower, the tower is your end, and your means will probably be a combination of walking, driving and flying.

When you're booking your trip (means), you'll examine your options based on what's important to you; flight duration, arrival time, legroom and so on.

You could call these your values; they're guiding your choices (means) towards your goal (end).

One of my big bugbears about the word "value," is that it's become an expression of both means and end. It's a bit confusing, so let's take your home as an example.

If you own your home, it's valuable; it increases your net worth, you can borrow against it, and you can put more money into it to increase its value (means).

But you don't buy a property just to store value; you want a secure and stable home to bring up your children, enjoy your leisure time or its proximity to restaurants and nightlife (ends).

You don't value it as an asset, you "value" it as a home, for the lifestyle it provides. It's a means to your end.

You can see we need another word to describe our values.

Fortunately for us, the Ancient Philosophers are once more on hand to help out with the concept of "Virtue".

While Virtue has grown a veneer of morality (good/bad or right/wrong), its original meaning was to develop excellence of character.

Our Ancient Philosophers believed developing excellence in beauty was just as virtuous as developing excellence in building houses. It was the effort of devoting your lifetime to becoming something more that was important.

Some people, and particularly businesses, use values to guide their goals and work. That seems reasonable, but so often the values are nebulous concepts like "respect", "integrity", "teamwork" and "accountability".

These concepts often come with definitions that limit their applicability, and that's reasonable too because value is a fixed point.

Any Realtor can give you a "value" for your house, but you won't know what it's worth until you sell it.

Nor will you know what "respect" really means until you're in a position to challenge that business, for example, trying to get a refund for your Paris plane tickets.

Ancient Virtues, on the other hand, are works in progress. You get to define both your means and ends knowing they're movable and each is a step towards something bigger.

Essentially, your Virtues are your means of bringing your vision and mission (ends) alive. They're your road map, or these days your Global Positioning System (GPS).

Once you plug in your destination, your GPS calculates your route and rules out all the options that don't get you where you want to go.

And if you lose focus and get lost, it gently suggests you "turn around where possible" so you can get back on track.

You can have as many Virtues as you want, but they'll be easier to develop and incorporate into your life if you can keep them down to a reasonable number.

What's reasonable depends on you, but most life coaches and advisers recommend somewhere between three and seven.

Each Virtue is both a core belief and a decision-making criterion relevant to your life right now. And like the other statements, you'll want to personalise it for your situation and revise it annually.

For example, if one of your Virtues is Honesty, you are committing to telling the truth in all circumstances. This may be difficult, particularly if you don't like hurting people's feelings. But if you hope for a career in politics, being known for telling the truth could be an asset.

Courage might translate into a career in the military, a commitment to visiting a dentist twice a year, or simply getting the spiders out of the bath yourself.

Simplicity could mean decluttering, less complicated financial arrangements or following a weekly menu plan.

Virtues are also opportunities for personal development so you can choose attributes you want to grow into, like Calm, Joy or Openness. And of course, you can describe these in a meaningful way.

If you look back through the Family visions and missions, you'll see they share themes, and these are an indication of where their Virtues lie.

Baker

While Emily wants marriage and a family someday, her statements suggest Independence, Prosperity and Freedom are important to her in the short term. If she was inclined, she might add Affection and Friendship, or just leave it at three virtues for the moment. She could go a little further and define what they look like for the next couple of years, for example, Independence could mean developing self-reliance, or Prosperity learning about wealth management.

Smith

Clearly, Bob and Amanda think Family is the most important, and following (or because of) this, Health, Education, and Community or perhaps Connection.

Butcher

Ash and Jo have recognised they're in danger of losing touch with each other, and want to make their relationship their top priority so their first Virtue may be Love, Relationship, or Romance. And as they want to work on it together, another could be Teamwork. They have a focus on cooking and an activity requiring a high level of fitness so they could round it out with Health or Well-being.

What Alexandria does

I went public with my planning a couple of years back. You can find it here https://www.alexandriablaelock.com/project-life-worth-living/.

Summary

Your Vision, Mission and Virtues provide a guidance system helping you establish and enjoy a life worth living.
- Your vision statement describes your ideal universe in a five to ten-year framework.
- Your mission statement explains what you're going to do in the next three years to get part of the way there.
- Your Virtues are your core beliefs, decision-making criteria and opportunities for personal development.

CHAPTER 2

Priorities

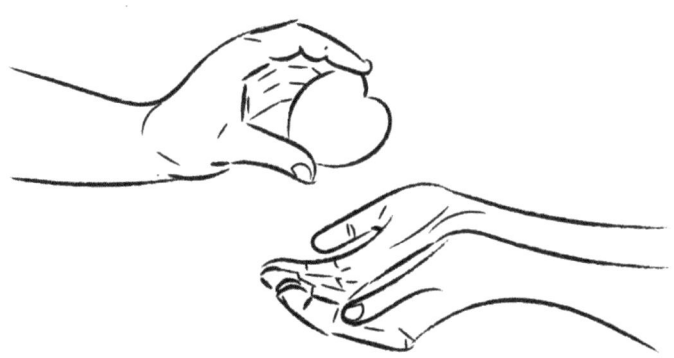

Planning a Life Worth Living

YOU MIGHT HAVE NOTICED I slotted the word priority in the Butcher's list of Virtues.

It used to be you could only have one priority - that there could only be one most important thing.

Now, however, we've moved to more of a ranking/precedence system.

And that's where I'm headed.

Virtues are a great basis for moving on and getting stuff done. But now and again, something comes up that seems, on balance, as important as some other thing, and you need a way to break the deadlock.

Your life is made up of stuff; tangible and intangible stuff.

Tangible is the stuff you can touch, like your dinner burning in the oven.

Intangible is the stuff you can't, like remembering to put the oven timer on when you put your dinner in the oven.

It's also stuff you can't see, like your relationships.

Or time.

As you progress through any given day, you'll come across situations where you need to choose the appropriate action to take. And most commonly, it'll be something along the lines of choosing where to spend your time or money; your employer or a member of your family.

And then you might have to choose which project to work on, or what movie to go see. Not to mention the ongoing dilemma of taking care of your health.

Your priorities might also be virtues, or they could be smaller ideals, closer to home.

Common priorities are family, health, and work.

Others that might be meaningful for you include:
- god/spiritual growth,
- self-care
- community service

- friendship
- your sports team
- hobbies
- education
- financial freedom/independence
- lifestyle/balance/skills

If we look at our families;

Baker

Emily's moving out of home, paying off her debts and seeking Independence. She might prioritise paid overtime this year so she can pay off her student loans quicker. And as she's young, and thinks she's immortal, might make health the last thing in her decision making.

Smith

Bob and Amanda will most likely put their kids first. And as they want them to grow up big and strong, put Health second on the list. Or perhaps Bob wants a promotion and may put his work second.

Butcher

Ash and Jo are making their relationship number one, and health number two.

So having explained priorities, in general, there will always be times when they get blown out of the water by a job or some other thing that becomes the most important thing.

It's fine to reshuffle now and again, when a deadline is approaching, or someone you know needs your support.

And at those times you might need to just drop everything and focus on that one thing.

Depending on your circumstances at the time, it might be possible to drop, or reschedule one or two goals until your circumstances change back.

When the time comes to choose, one of the most important questions you need to ask yourself, is whether you'd regret it:
- Not dropping everything to fly cross country to take care of your mother.
- Not taking that big new job offer.
- Not taking one last try at saving your marriage.

And you're the only person who can choose that, in the context of your Vision, Mission and Virtues.

What Alexandria Does

As for me, I had to quit paid work a decade ago due to ill health, and I now have a transplanted organ to take care of. I'm fortunate to have been married to the same person for almost a quarter of a century (though tomorrow I might change my mind about that!) And as well as writing books, I do a little editing and writing for other people. My priorities this year:

Family

Because despite what I said above, I'm quite fond of my husband, and I'd like to stay married to him.

And at the risk of inflating his ego, my day really does revolve around him - I schedule my paid and unpaid work around his comings and goings.

Not to mention, that if anything happens to me I'll need him to get me the help I require.

Health

By which I mean eating, drinking, sleeping, moving and de-stressing. Obviously I have the health of the transplant to worry about, though that doesn't prevent me from making unwise choices from time to time.

But in general I try to eat fresh food, limit salt and sugar, drink water while I still can, and aim for 7 - 8 hours' sleep a night. I know I don't move as much as I should, but I prefer to walk and take public transport so it's not all bad.

I manage my workload as much as I can to reduce the stress of deadlines. I also make all my medical and dental appointments way ahead of time, and work around them. Plus schedule lunches with friends, and give myself days off to unwind.

Work

Work is a tricky one for me, because I love my work, and I need to constrain it rather than do more of it. I try to shut down my computer and move into Family mode at 5:30 pm.

Though I get restless when I don't write, and if I don't write for long enough, my muse looks for someone else to play with. So the payoff there is that I write every day.

Leisure

Free time is important, and we'll often go to shows or events on Sundays. I like to visit Farmer's Markets as well, partly to top up my Artistic Well, and partly for fresh food.

Plus I read a lot (for fun as well as research) and watch movies (the same). Now and again I'll walk to my local shops for a latte to watch and listen to people. But at the same time, I know I have to leave the reading and tv watching until after the work is done, or nothing gets done.

Summary

- Priorities help you rank competing issues that seem equally important.
- They might be Virtues, or smaller ideals closer to home.
- Priorities can and do change as your life changes.

CHAPTER 3

Goals

As far as I'm concerned, one of the key components of a happy life is setting and achieving goals. You'll feel like you're getting somewhere, but the crucial thing is knowing where your particular somewhere is.

Which is why I suggested you start with a Vision (five years), a Mission (three years) and now Goals (one year).

A goal, is something you can achieve within the time you allow yourself. I'm focusing on annual goals because our lives to date have been counted out by years; birthdays, school years and workplace reviews. And those big New Year celebrations.

The same principles apply to goals of any duration, (e.g., a month or decade). The difference is in how you achieve them.

Goal Setting

There are several frameworks you can use to put together your goals, depending on what they are.

SMART Goals

The most common advice is to set SMART goals:
- **Specific:** Or well defined. Not just to travel, but to sail around the world.
- **Measurable:** You have an indicator of progress. Your trip is made of smaller tasks (e.g., getting your passport and visas, travel vaccinations, and arranging pet accommodation). You can tick each of these steps off as your departure date comes closer.
- **Achievable:** You can do it. If you get seasick, sailing probably won't work. You may be better cruising on a monster ocean liner or taking a bus.
- **Realistic:** Is within the scope of your available knowledge, time and resources. You have access to

a sailboat and can go for a significant period of time without a regular income.
- **Timely:** The amount of time required is not too much or too little; for example, you're not trying to circumnavigate the world in a fortnight.

SMART goals can be quite difficult, especially if you hope to develop a new Virtue.

Let's say you decided to cultivate the Virtue of Honesty, you may have to get creative.

- **S:** Be honest with one person, or about one issue.
- **M:** Note the number of times you were tempted to lie, and the number of times you told the truth.
- **A:** Give yourself some learner leeway, and be honest maybe 75% of the time.
- **R:** You do have the ability to tell the truth, you just have to want to.
- **T:** This year.

It kind of works, doesn't it? But it may be better to use a different approach.

HARD Goals

Life is messy and held together by passion. Life goals don't always fit into a neat objective framework. They may be better expressed as HARD goals.

- **Heartfelt:** You have a strong emotional attachment to the outcome.
- **Animated:** You can vividly imagine and connect to it.
- **Required:** They are absolutely necessary for success.
- **Difficult:** You need to learn, develop new skills, and grow as a person.

So, looking again at Honesty;

- **H:** You're really tired of being a lying douche bag.
- **A:** You can visualise trust building and relationships deepening.
- **R:** You can't live a happy life without interacting with other people.
- **D:** It's like a leopard changing its spots.

"Better" Goals

Sometimes neither SMART nor HARD goals are right. Sometimes you just want to do better than last year. To speak Spanish more proficiently, read more books, or improve your focus.

These kinds of goals are the best for developing Virtues. They're also a little gentler when you fail - rather than calling yourself a dishonest loser, you take comfort from being more honest than you were before.

Rather than getting depressed about your "failure" and giving up, you can take a break, consider what strategies may be more useful, and start afresh.

Longer Term Goals

Some annual goals will be part of a larger plan. For example, our student whose mission was to "Help sick animals by getting good grades and becoming a veterinarian" has automatically set an annual goal of passing their exams until they graduate as a vet licenced to practice. But for this year, they could set themselves a minimum grade of 85%.

Stretch Goals

Ordinarily, goals should be achievable, but, some people like to set themselves "stretch" goals. These goals are so ambitious they're seemingly impossible.

Which can be very de-motivating if you're not passionate about the outcome, but if you are, they can inspire you to go to extraordinary lengths to achieve them.

For you to achieve this goal, your end must fully justify your means.

Our veterinary student, for example, might set a grade goal of 99.55%, which will require extreme dedication to achieve. They must learn to study more efficiently and effectively. They'll probably irritate their instructors and fellow students with their constant questions. They'll have to sacrifice leisure time for more hands-on practice and may lose friends.

Wealth Management Goals

Your life goals, guided by your vision, mission and virtues, give you the opportunity to choose where to cut spending to give yourself the best chance of achieving your goals.

For example, given the goal of sailing around the world, you might cut all your spending back to the bare minimum to maximise your savings so you can travel for longer (which will also put you in the habit of spending less which will help you to preserve your funds for longer).

Or if you're developing Honesty, you might reduce your clothing spend to allow for more apology gifts for the people you offend. Only you can decide whether your sacrifices are worth their cost.

Living a happier life requires a delicate balance. You have to manage the cost of achieving your goals without sacrificing your mental, physical or spiritual requirements.

If Family is one of your Virtues, and you're too tired or thinking too hard about work when you get home to enjoy your time with them, you need to consider whether your work supports your vision or needs to change.

You could buy in help to get more time with your family, or acknowledge that right now (but not forever) it's more important to work so you can get more secure housing even if it does cost you time with your family.

But back to the goal setting.

Like virtues, you can have as many goals as you like, but the more goals you have, the harder it is to achieve them.

Seemingly Warren Buffet advises an elimination strategy. First, write down the top 25 things you want to do, then work on the top five, ignoring the rest until the top five are done.

Every moment you spend tinkering with the bottom 20 is a moment you're not working towards what you really want.

Because goals are built on your vision for the future, you may find goals for one virtue have flow on effects for others. If our Honest person also has the Virtue of Discipline, every time they tell the truth and strengthen the Virtue of Honesty, they reinforce the Virtue of Discipline at the same time.

Similarly, our veterinary student probably has the Virtue of Caring in addition to Education, so by pursuing opportunities to care for animals they develop both.

Let's take a look at what our families could do. For the sake of page numbers (and book price), I'll illustrate one goal each.

Baker

With her vision of independence, and mission of an Abundant future, Emily's discovered apartment rentals range from $500 - $1,000 per month, with establishment costs about the same. Before she signs a lease, she wants to practice paying rent so she (and her parents) can be assured it's affordable; she'll be attempting to save the equivalent of rent each month.

She wants to move somewhere nice (and safe), and will stretch her monthly savings goal to $1,100. At the end of the year, she'll have achieved the habit of living on less and saved her deposit and first month's rent.

She'll also have $13,200 she can use to buy homewares, take a trip, or pay down her student loans.

Her SMART goal becomes: "This year, I'll bank $1,100 each month in a high-interest savings account."

Smith

With the vision of moving to a cleaner, close-knit community and the mission of prioritising the children's interests, the Smiths decide it's time to move. While they want to do it NOW, they agree it's for the long-term, and they must be sure it's the right place. They decide to research what they need, and where their needs can be met.

Their HARD goal is "We'll shortlist five potential communities by the end of the year."

Butcher

Ash and Jo want to focus on the Virtues of Love, Teamwork and Health by cooking a meal together at home once a week.

Their GET BETTER goal becomes "We'll grow our relationship by preparing and eating healthy food together."

Summary

- Goals are steps towards achieving your mission and bringing your ideal universe into being.
- They can be SMART, HARD, or Better.
- Setting lifestyle goals helps prioritise spending and manage wealth.

CHAPTER 4

Clarity

Planning a Life Worth Living

ONCE UPON A TIME, I worked as a Personal Assistant. Which led to becoming an Executive Assistant, then a Project Manager and a bit later, a Programme Manager.

Project/Programme Managers generally manage what you might consider extreme goals:

- Events like weddings, tennis tournaments, or international peace treaties.
- Constructions like family houses, highways, or rail lines.
- IT like phone apps, system upgrades, or new customer management systems.

Your successful Project Management career depends on delivering a project that does what it's supposed to do, on time and on, or under budget.

And it's really easy for time and cost to escalate out of control if you don't keep on top of them.

So, when I'm managing a project, I needed something to give me clarity about what I was doing. An objective to keep me focused, and on track. Something along the lines of:

Achieve some end at a particular cost by a specified date.

So that might end up as

- Hold a Steampunk themed wedding for 100 guests for $10,000 on July 15.
- Buy and install a fancy new customer management system that seamlessly integrates with existing inventory and logistic systems for $100,000 before Christmas.
- Build 10 km of highway, including relevant over and underground sections and complementary landscaping for $1,000,000 within two years.

All of these statement tell you the time, cost and quality you're aiming to achieve. If if starts to look like you're not going to meet one of key criteria, you can choose which of the others to sacrifice to stay on track:
- increase costs by getting more people on the job
- use the same resources but take longer.
- reduce the costs by reducing the quality.

Or, if your circumstances change, and it seems to difficult to continue, to dump the whole thing and do something else.

Summary

- A Statement of Objective reminds you of the time, cost and quality you're aiming for.
- It can help you stay on track to achieve the outcome you want.
- It can help you make informed decisions about changes you may need to make to get there.

CHAPTER 5

Planning

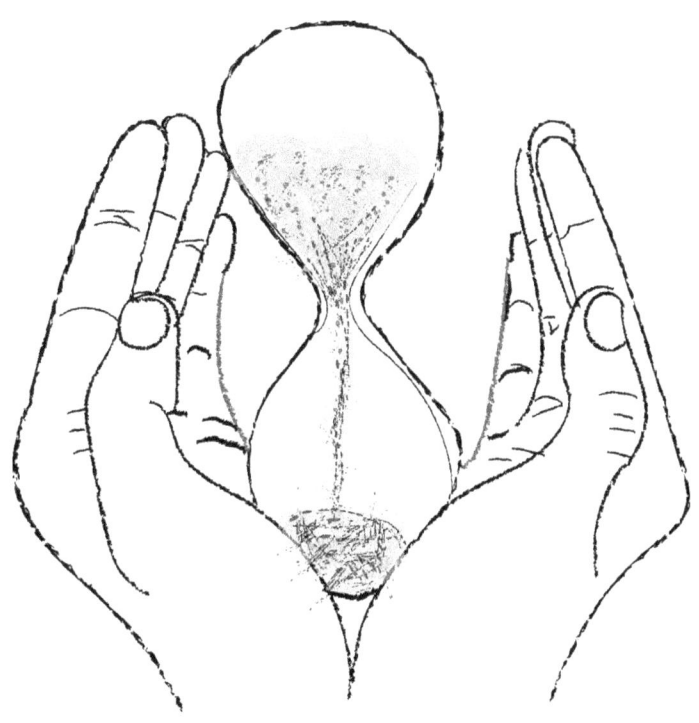

Planning a Life Worth Living

SETTING AND CLARIFYING GOALS ISN'T the end of the story - you won't achieve your goals if you don't lay out a plan for reaching them.

Most people who don't make plans forget and abandon their goals by the end of the month they make them.

A plan is a bit like the recipe you use to make a meal. It's a list of ingredients and steps you need to take (your means) bring about the result you want (your end).

The ky components are a time frame, and a budget (or as I call them, spending plan).

In this chapter I'll mainly be talking about scheduling because I wrote a lot about money in *Holistic Personal Finance*. And in most cases, saving an amount of money each pay is generally enough to cover the costs.

Planning out your schedule is what makes the sheer variety of tasks achievable within the time allowed.

Your Paris trip or University curriculum might involve a plan that lasts a year or two. Christmas might take eleven months to buy and post everything you need. Some meeting hosts think you can cram two hours of meeting into one.

Like any heroine dealing with her arch nemesis, it helps to have a plan. Here's what our families migh do.

Baker

Emily's is relatively straightforward; she can open a dedicated savings account and have part of her pay deposited into it. She could even make it an account that's harder to withdraw from, for example, one without an ATM card, or where she has to wait 24 hours for the funds to be transferred to her everyday account.

Smith

The Smiths have accidentally set themselves an enormous goal. The best way to proceed is to break the bigger goal into smaller steps within a logical framework. They should agree some responsibilities and time frames and add them to their calendars to make sure they progress their goal.

For example, start by deciding some respectful communication ground rules. Allowing a month to agree their "must have" and "nice to have" attributes, and another to identify preferred and no-go countries or states. After a year of investigating the relative merits and cost of living in each area, they can rank them and pick their preferred location.

Butcher

Ash and Jo's goal is both easy and hard at the same time. They need to find some local classes at times they can both make, and schedule these along with Date Night as priority weekly appointments. They'll need a conscious, ongoing focus (e.g., packing up and leaving work "early") until it becomes an automatic response.

Scheduling the Year

I find that a good plan is like a drawing. You start with the broad strokes, then fill in the smaller details.

And I don't like having multiple calendars, so I prefer to keep one main calendar with *everything* on it. All my business and personal goals, appointments, and to-dos.

Of course I'm lucky because I'm self employed and I can do that, but you may be juggling a variety of scheduling tools across multiple work sites. If possible, pick one app to be your main and synchronise the others to it.

Start scheduling your fixed and immovable appointments, deadlines and tasks such as birthdays, medical appointments and academic dates.

Then look at how you can leverage the effort you're investing in them towards other ends, for example, scheduling as many personal appointments as you can on your rostered day off, or in the same general location.

Regardless of how you do it, make the schedule fit your circumstances, not the other way around.

Your Longer-Term Schedule

You might not know it, but you have regular commitments taking place over a time-frame longer a year.

These activities are more like major projects, generally in the form of household maintenance like replacing furnaces and water heaters or repainting your window trims.

It can also include medical care like repeat tests and vaccinations, or replacement fillings and implants.

I am aware it seems like overkill to plan an event that won't happen for a decade, but if you don't have some kind of bring forward system, it's likely you'll forget.

And while it sounds like you'll probably be fine, but what if it's replacing your water heater? You might find when it breaks down, you don't have the funds to replace it. Or there might not be stock on hand so you may have to wait for several days for one to come in. Or installation may be delayed. Much better to have a note to remind yourself in nine and a half years to replace it before it breaks down.

Annual Schedule

You also have an annual plan, which is most recognisable in birthdays, religious observances and sales shopping. It's useful to start adding in tasks like servicing your climate control, replacing small appliances and testing the market to see if your insurances (etc.) are still the best ones for you.

It's also excellent for planning out the actions you need to take to achieve those New Year's goals; allocate them to seasons, then to months and weeks.

Quarterly Schedule

Similarly, you may have a quarterly schedule, probably in the form of seasonal preparations such as preparing for the Summer bushfire or Winter storm seasons. Or your Spring and Autumn wardrobe swaps.

You might also like to think of the seasonality of your paid and unpaid work. What impacts the weather, local events, and holiday seasons will have on the schedule.

Monthly Schedule

You may also have some form of monthly schedule - many activities such as farmers markets and professional development happen on a rotating monthly calendar, (e.g., the second Tuesday or third Sunday).

Even if you don't, you might like to use a monthly schedule for rotating cycles of work. Cleaning is the easiest example; dust daily, wipe greasy weekend fingerprints off the furniture on Mondays, and on the last Monday of each month, lovingly polish your wood furniture with beeswax.

Sometimes a monthly schedule is useful for longer term projects such as weight loss with a cycle of food and exercise management.

Weekly Schedule

Similarly, you probably already have some kind of regular schedule tied to external drivers at home and work, such as your rubbish collection, Tuesday evening football practice or Friday morning video conferences to the office.

These commitments can generally slot into your daily schedule, with other tasks layered around them, though now and again you'll need to rearrange to attend external appointments or take care of bigger jobs like storm clean up.

When you hit those kind of days, try not to stress too much about your schedule. Check to see what else is on, and consider what you can skip and what needs to be rescheduled.

Daily Schedule

One of the easiest ways to get things done, is to start with a daily plan, and there are two main ways to do this; time blocking and the ideal day.

Time Blocking

Time blocking is the process of blocking out several consecutive hours of time to work on groups of work rather than individual tasks.

For example, Monday mornings for planning, or Thursday afternoons for marketing.

You'll see it most commonly when you block half a day for a particular meeting, but you can do the same thing for tackling projects.

It's useful when you want to do some sustained work on a project, or you have lots of small tasks you don't want to schedule individually.

It works with a time management technique called batching, where you spend a period of time working on one task, for example answering email, or data entry.

If you are using a group calendar, you might like to mark your private appointments as something cryptic (e.g., lunch dates as NoMS), private or Do Not Disturb.

Your Ideal Day

An ideal day is completely unachievable, broad outline of the kind of day where everything goes right, and you get everything done you need to, so it makes a good basic template for planning out your tasks.

It has a start and a finish, and you get a lunch break. And because it's ideal, it takes advantage of your high and low energy times.

For example, you might spend the first hour of your day responding to email, the next couple of hours meeting with your staff. Then a spot of lunch, some filing, and organising a forum you're planning.

And while I call it an ideal day, you can have different kinds of ideal days for different kinds of circumstances. For example, I have an ideal for when I start researching and writing new books. And I have a different kind of ideal day for when I move into editing and publishing.

If daily doesn't work for you, you could have an "ideal week" instead.

The "Right" Time

If you're not sure when your right time for uninterrupted work is, Dan Pink is here to help out. In his book *When: The Scientific Secrets of Perfect Timing* he tells us in general, our mood rises in the morning, dips in the afternoon and rises again in the evening.

The exact timing depends on what your chronotype is - morning people are at their peak in the morning, and unsurprisingly, night owls are at theirs at night. Interestingly, trying to work outside your hours can be as hard as trying to work at the legal alcohol limit!

Planning a Life Worth Living

However, in general, it's best to do analytic work in your chronotype's "morning" when you're fresh, and your creative work in the chronotype afternoon. Or the important stuff at your peak, and the second most important in your recovery.

And when I say your important stuff, I mean do the work you get paid for at your peak, and the work you don't get paid for in the slump.

You can also use this information for planning your time blocks, equipment services, deliveries and external appointments. Or helping you schedule naps and rearrange your work when you take days off.

Minor Tasks in the Schedule

Your schedule usually only includes the large regularly occurring jobs. But you know there are little tasks, like putting your tools away or emptying the kitchen bin that happen frequently but not regularly.

They're not usually the kind of thing you schedule, you'll usually stack them into your existing habits (e.g., put your tools away when you finish the job).

You can also plan activities to minimise future disruptions, for example, shopping to ensure deliveries occur at regular, predictable times, and you've sufficient cash on hand to pay or tip for it as it arrives.

Summary

- Use an "Ideal Day" for your planning framework.
- Plan around your existing commitments.
- Include short, medium, and long-term commitments.

CHAPTER 6

Tracking

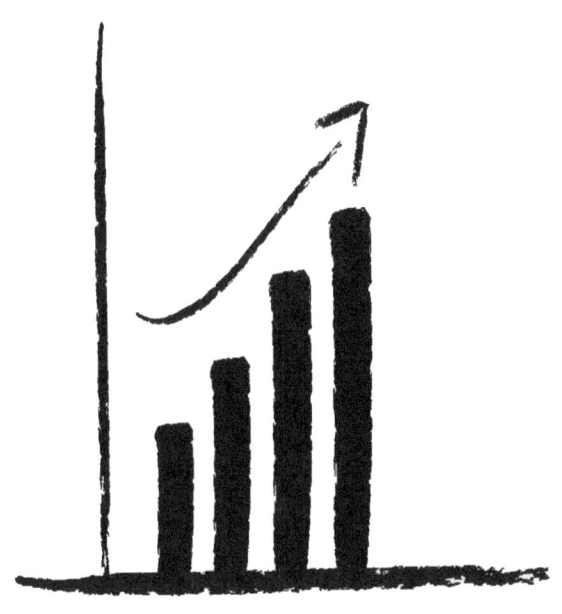

SETTING GOALS IS ONE THING, keeping them is another.

Especially as most goals are set at about five to midnight on New Year's Eve after too much champagne.

Mind you, even with a plan, it's really easy to get distracted by life and forget about your goals or veer off track.

You need to check in now and again to see how you are proceeding with your goals.

Some of them will be as easy as checking off each glass of water as you drink it, or book as you read it. Others, like weddings, require a bit more thought.

The easiest way is to set a time line, add it to your calendar, and check it off as you go.

If you start falling behind, or getting too far ahead, consider whether you need to change your goal or your process.

And if you choose to finish the goal, think about what you can replace it with.

Monthly Tracking

Essentially, you're going to look at the plan to see whether you're on time and on budget.

You are? That's great?

You're ahead? That's great too.

If you're behind, or the costs are blowing out, you've got some decisions to make.

Let's go back to our chapter four example, the Steampunk themed wedding for 100 guests for $10,000 on July 15, and it looks like it's going to cost more.

The Wedding

Once a wedding juggernaut builds up speed, it's impossible to slow down, so unless you're very early in your planning you won't be able to change the date.

Which leaves you the options
- reduce costs
- increase the budget

The first option to consider is always to reduce costs. In the case of a wedding, there are lots of ways to reduce costs; the venues, the catering, the cake, the flowers, the dresses, the cars, the invitations (etc.) as well as inviting fewer guests.

When you consider that the average wedding costs $25,000 - $35,000 (which would also make a nice house deposit), and is generally financed by debt rather than savings, you might prefer not to increase the budget.

In fact, as a general principle, I'd advise you to consider very carefully before you increase the budget.

The Customer Management System

This one's a bit businessy, but where you're buying and installing a customer management system that seamlessly integrates with existing inventory and logistic systems for $100,000 before Christmas you're faced with a different problem.

While it would be great to have it by Christmas, in terms of increased efficiency, it's more important that it seamlessly integrates with the existing systems. So in this case, we'd probably be prepared to spend a little more and wait and a little longer.

The Highway

When it comes to the 10 km of highway, including relevant over and underground sections and complementary landscaping for $1,000,000 within two years, it gets easier and more complex at the same time.

With so many tasks to complete, it may be possible to work on the overpass while doing the landscaping and reduce the time line.

Or hire additional people at additional cost to crush the time line.

Or buy more smaller plants to reduce costs.

Most Likely Scenario

Having said all that, it's more likely your plans are running behind schedule. Mainly because you have no idea how long any of your goals is really going to take.

How long does it take me to write a book? The fastest for me was about a month, and the longest about eleven. How long does the editing take? How long laying out the book and designing the covers?

How long will it take you to learn the guitar? With weekly lessons, and daily practice maybe three months, maybe more. How good do you have to get to consider that you've learnt the guitar? Maybe you'll be good enough to jam with your besties after three months, but if you want to join an orchestra it could take years. Or maybe you'll hate it and give it up before your fingertips harden up.

So what you'll end up doing each month, is considering whether the effort you're putting into your goals each month is worth it.

- Have you reached the level of expertise you want, or do you need to keep working?
- Are you invested enough in the goal to keep it up for another month, or is it time to quit?
- Are you prepared to keep saving up or investing in the goal for another month? Would you prefer to save/pay more for another month, or less?

Quarterly Tracking

Sometimes, monthly can be too often to track, in which case once a quarter might be better.

In any case, if your annual goal is blowing out, you should consider recalculating the steps you need to get to your goal.

Let's say you've given yourself one year to drop 15 kg, losing 300g per week. At the end of the quarter, you've only lost 2 kg, and have fallen 1.75 kg behind.

You could double down and try to lose 360g/week and try to meet your original goal. Or you could continue at 300g/week and meet your goal over a longer term.

Annual Tracking

At the end of the year, you'll be considering how you went. Did you achieve you goal? If not, will you abandon it or bring it into the next year?

In any case, it will help your next goals if you take some time to assess how you went.

- What went well?
- What didn't go well?
- What will you do differently next time?
- Did you learn anything you can apply to other situations.

Summary

Ask yourself if your goal is contributing to a worthwhile life.
- Is it worth putting in the time and cost?
- Are you progressing as well as you hoped?

Conclusion

GETTING ORGANISED, AND GETTING THINGS done has been a matter of trial and error for me.

I look back with some fondness on the time when I didn't have anything that needed to go in my diary aside from a few birthdays. I spent more time choosing them than I did writing in them.

But as time went by, life got more complicated, and I started missing important events. Like that one job interview...

So be aware that this system might not work for you without a bit of tweaking.

Especially if you don't capture the details; like reminding yourself to buy the birthday gift before it's due.

And even if it does, without the right kind of diary and bring forward system, it can still get messed up.

For me, that's one notebook, a kind of bullet journal, productivity diary, with photos and ticket stubs and stuff. You can read more about it here https://www.alexandriablaelock.com/productivity-journalling/

Planning a Life Worth Living

For others that might be a printed calendar in the kitchen, a printed diary on the desk, and an electronic diary for work.

Or maybe something like Trello, Asana or Kanboard.

Just like the goals, you need to find your why before you find your how.

Good luck!

Glossary

End: the result you want, for example, to be in Spain. See also Means.

Flourishing: an awareness of growing and developing, reaching to become more than you were before.

Ideal Day: a time management concept of the perfect working day that takes advantage of your natural high and low energy periods includes time for uninterrupted work, and all your tasks are completed quickly and easily. It's not really possible to achieve, but you plan your normal days according to the Ideal Day template.

Means: any method for getting what you want (your end), for example, taking an aeroplane to get to Spain. See also End.

NaNoWriMo: National Novel Writing Month, a challenge to wrote 50,000 words during the month of November. For more, see https://nanowrimo.org/.

Virtue: a centre of excellence, an important skill or attitude that takes a lot of time and effort to get good at.

Bibliography

Blaelock, Alexandria. 2018. *Minimally Viable Housekeeping.* Melbourne: BlueMere Books.

Blaelock, Alexandria. 2020. *Holistic Personal Finance.* Melbourne: BlueMere Books.

Kant, Immanuel. 1998. *Groundwork of the Metaphysics of Morals.* Cambridge. Cambridge University Press.

Pink, Daniel. 2018. *When: The scientific secrets of perfect timing.* Melbourne: Text Publishing.

Index

Annual
    scheduling......................... 36
    tracking 45
Baker
    goals 26
    mission statement 9
    planning 34
    priorities 17
    virtues statement 13
    vision statement 7
Blaelock
    priorities 18
    vision, mission, virtues .. 14
Butcher
    goals 27
    mission statement 9
    planning 35
    priorities 17
    virtues statement 13
    vision statement 8
Daily scheduling
    ideal day 39
    right time 39
    time blocking 38
Goal Setting 22
    better 24
    HARD 23
    longer term 24
    SMART 22
    stretch 24
    wealth management 25
Goals
    Baker 26
    Butcher 27
    Smith 27
Mission Statement 9
    Baker 9
    Butcher 9
    Smith 9
Monthly
    scheduling......................... 37
    tracking 42
Planning
    Baker 34
    Butcher 35
    Smith 34
Priorities
    Baker 17
    Butcher 17
    Smith 17
Quarterly
    scheduling 37
    tracking 45
Scheduling 35
    annual 36
    daily 38
    longer term 36
    minor tasks 40
    monthly 37
    quarterly 37
    weekly 37
Smith
    goals 27
    mission statement 9
    planning 34
    priorities 17
    virtues statement 13
    vision statement 7
Tracking
    annual 45
    monthly 42
    most likely scenario 44
    quarterly 45
Virtues Statement 10
    Baker 13
    Butcher 13
    Smith 13
Vision Statement 6
    Baker 7
    Butcher 8
    Smith 7

Author's Note

Thanks again for buying my book.

I hope it helps you get more life in your life.

If you'd like to let me know what you think, or share how you got on, drop me a line at hello@alexandriablaelock.com.

For more, visit me at alexandriablaelock.com to:

- read my blog

- check out my planning at alexandriablaelock.com/project-life-worth-living/

- sign up for *Letters from my Library* to stay up to date on the development and release of my books. You'll also get research interestingness (that doesn't get to the blog), gossip about my writing life, and the odd special offer.

About the Author

Alexandria Blaelock writes self-help books applying business techniques to personal matters like getting dressed, cleaning house, and feeding your friends. As a recovering Project Manager, she's probably too fond of sticking to plan.

She also writes short stories, some of them for *Ellery Queen's Mystery Magazine* and *Pulphouse Fiction Magazine*.

When not writing, she watches K-dramas, talks to animals, and drinks Campari. At the same time.

Discover more at www.alexandriablaelock.com.

www.ingramcontent.com/pod-product-compliance
Lightning Source LLC
Chambersburg PA
CBHW062113280426
43661CB00086B/630